MW00962239

STEALING HOME

A Collection of Baseball Jargon
Cartoons

STEALING HOME

drawn by

BOB KAPHEIM

INTRODUCTION

Every profession and sport has its own jargon and slang terms to define that profession or sport. Baseball is loaded with terms like southpaw, Keystone combination, knuckle ball, screwball and hot corner. This book attempts to turn baseball jargon into cartoons. Three of these cartoons, "Stealing Home," "Poppin the Cork," and "Hot Corner" all took first place in cartoon competition. That success became the inspiration to create this book of baseball jargon cartoons. These cartoons will help baseball fans new and old understand baseball jargon and make the game more entertaining. Enjoy!

DEDICATION

Dedicated to baseball fans everywhere.

ACKNOWLEDGEMENT

Thanks to Larry Puhl for his technical assistance in publishing this book. Larry's help was invaluable.

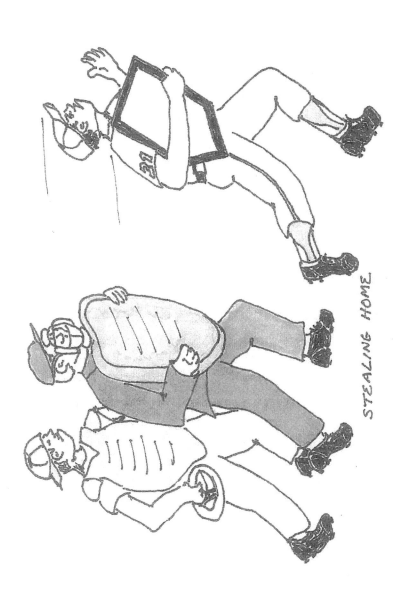

STEALING HOME

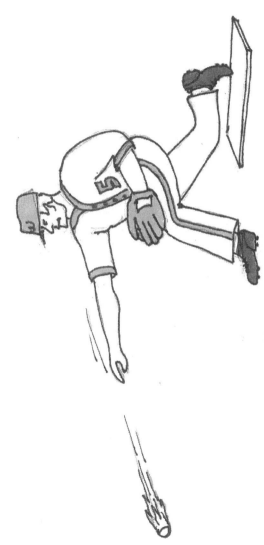

FIREBALLING RIGHT HANDER

PAINTING THE BLACK

PUNCH OUT

DOCTORING THE BALL

PULLED THE STRING

STANDING ON THE HILL

BRUSH BACK

WARMING UP IN THE BULL PEN

THROWING BEEBIES

PITCHER HAS A HOWITZER

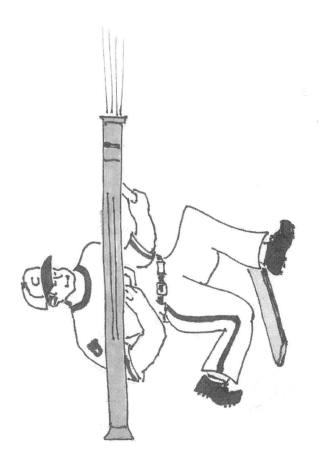

HE'S GOT A BAZOOKA FOR AN ARM

BEAN BALL PITCH

SET UP MAN

BATTERY MATES

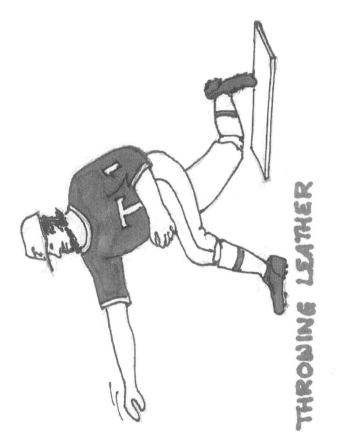

THROWING LEATHER

PITCH HAD SOME MUSTARD ON IT

GETTING the HOOK

BRINGING IN THE FIREMAN

SERVED ONE UP ON A PLATTER

SOUTH
PAW

NAILING DOWN A VICTORY

NAIL BITER

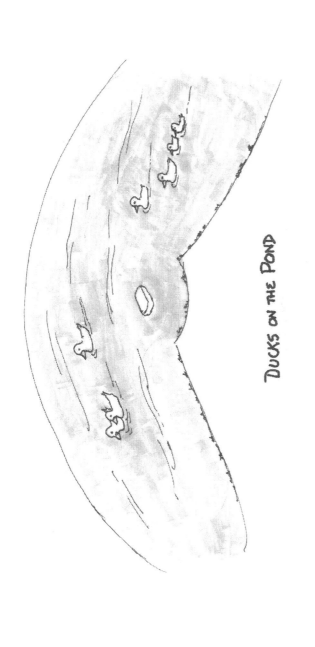

Ducks on the Pond

GOPHER BALL

MEAT BALL

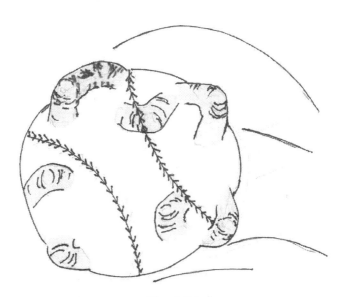

KNUCKLE BALL

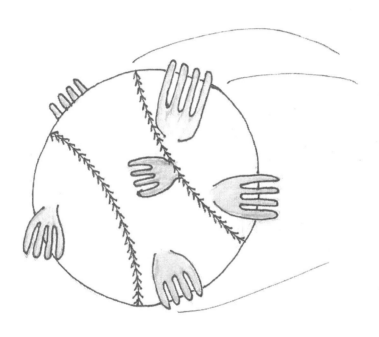

FORK BALL

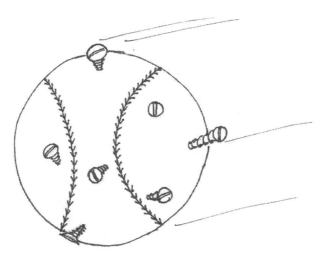

SCREW BALL

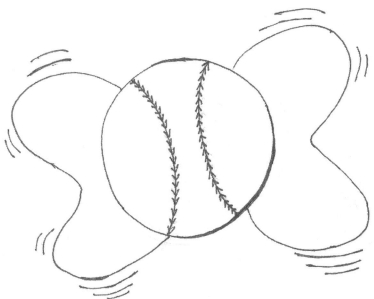

FLUTTER BALL

MONEY BALL

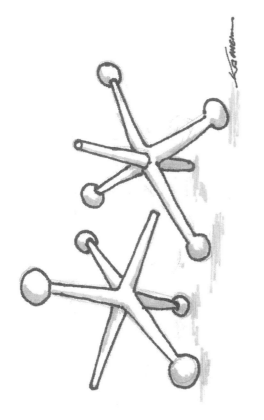

BACK TO BACK JACKS

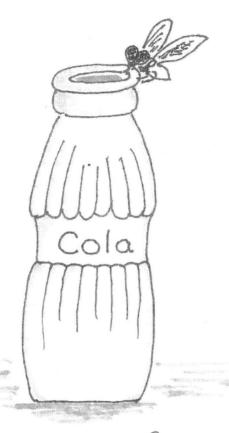

Cola

POP
FLY

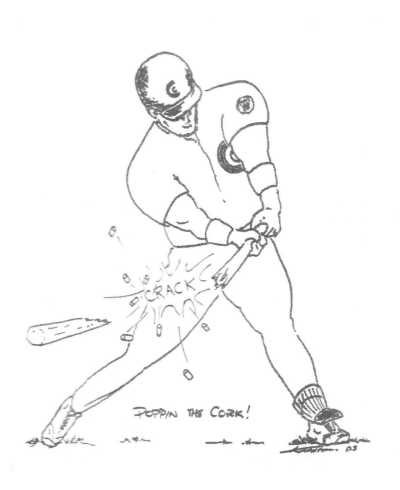

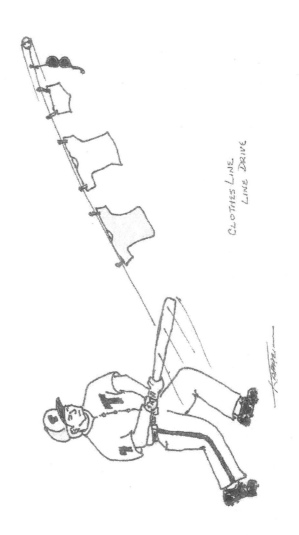

CLOTHES LINE
LINE DRIVE

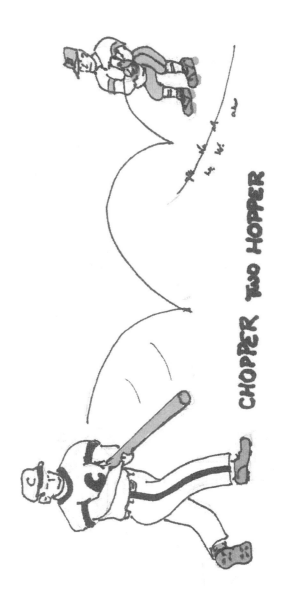

CHOPPER two HOPPER

FOULED BACK UP THE ELEVATOR

CURVE BALL DROPS OFF THE TABLE

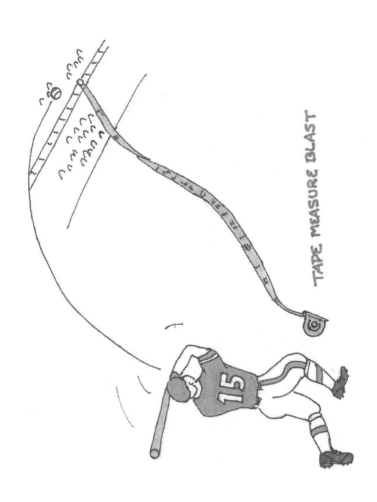

TAPE MEASURE BLAST

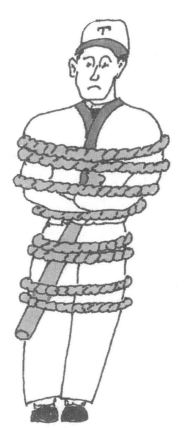

TIED HIM UP

SAWED THE BAT OFF IN HIS HANDS

HIT A BOMB

CUED THE BALL

STEPPING IN THE BUCKET

FREEZE the HITTER

HAMMERED THE BALL

SITTING IN THE CATBIRD'S SEAT

KNEE BUCKLER

DYING QUAIL

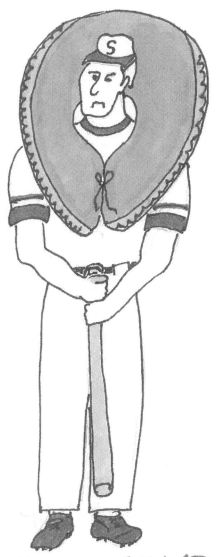

TOOK THE COLLAR

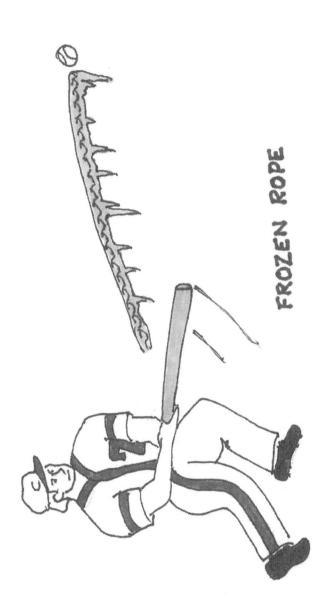

FROZEN ROPE

GOT A COOKIE TO HIT

BEHIND THE COUNT

CHIN MUSIC

HIT A BULLET

STEPPING UP TO THE DISH

MOON SHOT

HANDCUFFED THE BATTER

HIT ONE UP THE ALLEY

KNOCKED THE COVER OFF THE BALL

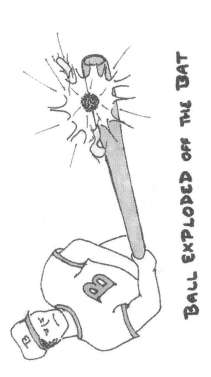

BALL EXPLODED OFF THE BAT

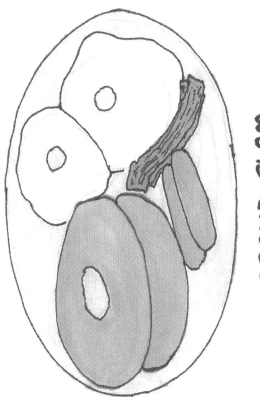

GRAND SLAM

PLAYER TO BE NAMED LATER

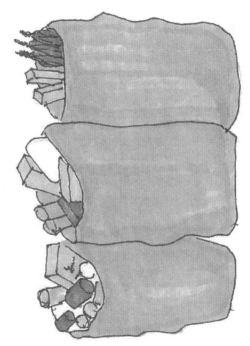

THE BAGS ARE LOADED

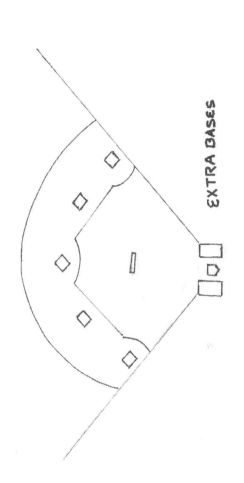

EXTRA BASES

TOOLS OF IGNORANCE

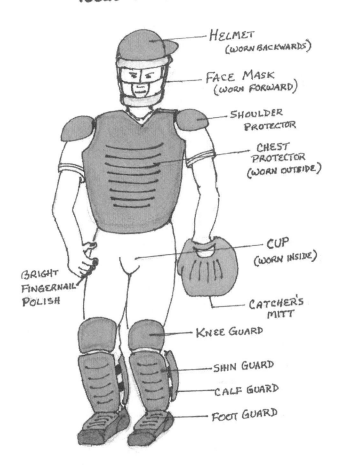

- HELMET (WORN BACKWARDS)
- FACE MASK (WORN FORWARD)
- SHOULDER PROTECTOR
- CHEST PROTECTOR (WORN OUTSIDE)
- CUP (WORN INSIDE)
- BRIGHT FINGERNAIL POLISH
- CATCHER'S MITT
- KNEE GUARD
- SHIN GUARD
- CALF GUARD
- FOOT GUARD

DUCK SNORT
FLY BALL

HOLE IN HIS GLOVE

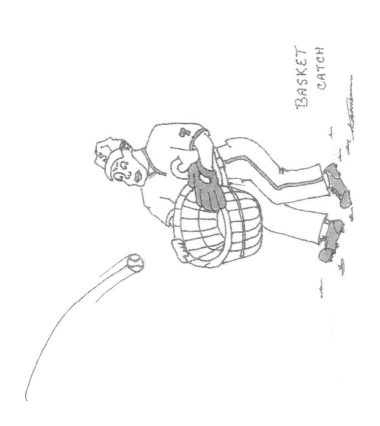

BASKET CATCH

CAUGHT NAPPING OFF FIRST

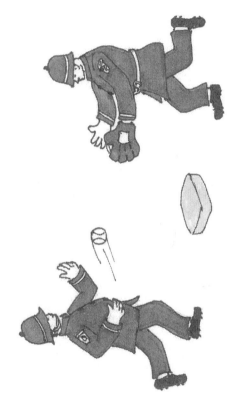

KEYSTONE COMBINATION

CAN of CORN

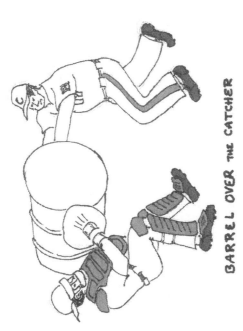

BARREL OVER THE CATCHER

FIVE TOOL PLAYER

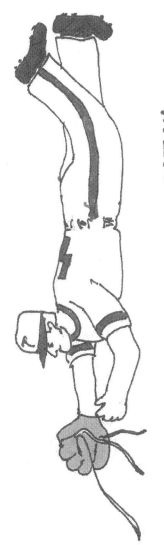

SHOE STRING CATCH

SNOW CONE

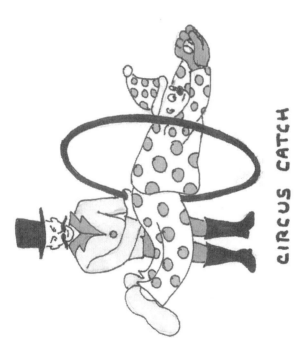

CIRCUS CATCH

BASEBALL'S 3RD BASE HOT CORNER

ABOUT the AUTHOR

Bob Kapheim is an award winning artists and photographer. He also designs and produces glass fusion pendants and dishes. Kapheim teaches drawing to individuals from third grade to senior citizens. He primarily draws with pencil, color pencil, charcoal, water color pencil, and pen and ink. This work is the result of pen and ink cartoons. Cartoons can serve as a metaphor for a concept or in this case baseball jargon. His work can be seen at www.bobsart71.com.

Dr. Bob Kapheim, during his career, has served as an educator, graduate instructor, presenter, consultant, and author. Kapheim formerly was an adjunct faculty member in the School of Education at Saint Xavier University in Chicago, Illinois. As an award winning educator he taught accelerated biology and general science at the high school level for thirty five years. In addition, he has taught ecology, environmental science, chemistry and physics. During his tenure as a secondary school teacher he won numerous awards including teacher of the year in his district, three national awards for innovative biology lessons, and was part of a delegation of biology teachers representing the United States in an exchange with Russia and Poland. He has been a presenter at national and state science and gifted conferences. Later he served as the Head of the Upper School and Dean at the Science and Arts Academy, a private school for gifted. While at the Science and Arts Academy he designed and installed the Interim, a highly innovative curriculum for gifted children. Bob began teaching graduate courses for Saint Xavier University through IRI Skylight. This experience led to his becoming the Director of Curriculum and Instruction for Pearson Education where he has managed field-based cohort Masters degree programs, discrete graduate level courses for Saint Xavier University, and distance education programs for both Saint Xavier and Drake University. Following his position at Pearson Education, Dr. Kapheim became the Dean of Math and Science at DeVry University in Addison, Illinois. As a consultant for IRI Skylight he has given programs throughout the United States on brain-based learning, multiple intelligence, cooperative education, authentic assessment, positive discipline, 20th Century education, instrumental enrichment, and Socratic Dialogue. Noted for his innovative curriculum designs, Dr. Kapheim has authored the book; "Question the Thought," which provides teachers with strategies for effective classroom discussion through Socratic Dialogue. In a departure from science, Dr. Kapheim authored a book entitled "Pardon My Bumper-Sticker," which is a cultural, anthropological study of the bumper-sticker that represents his first in a series of a social/cultural anthropological studies of the bumper-sticker culture in the United States. He recently authored "Cricket Creek," which is a book of essays on ecology and features 17 of his original drawings. This book was followed by a book based on those essays entitled, "Reading Exercises for Science." REfS was designed for teachers to help struggling readers in science. In 2015, Kapheim also published a cartoon book based on human pregnancy titled, "Autobiography of a Fetus." This book is ideal for a baby shower gift.

bobkapheim@yahoo.com

54110387R10049

Made in the USA
Charleston, SC
24 March 2016